Rootbound

Rootbound

Poems

Jeanne Emmons

Minnesota Voices Project
Number 84
New Rivers Press 1998

New Rivers Press is a nonprofit literary press dedicated to
publishing the very best emerging writers in our region,
nation, and world.

The publication of *Rootbound* has been made possible
by generous grants from the Jerome Foundation; the North
Dakota Council on the Arts; Target Stores, Dayton's,
and Mervyn's by the Dayton Hudson Foundation; and the
James R. Thorpe Foundation.

Additional support has been provided by the Elmer L.
and Eleanor J. Andersen Foundation, the Beim Foundation,
the General Mills Foundation, Liberty State Bank,
the McKnight Foundation, the Star Tribune/Cowles Media
Company, and the contributing members of
New Rivers Press.

New Rivers Press
420 North Fifth Street, Suite 910
Minneapolis, MN 55401

www.mtn.org/newrivpr

To my parents,
Winfred S. Emmons, Jr.,
and Ethel May Emmons

Contents

Acknowledgments

I gratefully acknowledge the publications in which some of the poems in *Rootbound* have previously appeared: "Maraschino Cherries at the A&P" in *Calyx, A Journal of Art and Literature by Women*, Summer 1997, vol. 17, no. 2. "Poppies Opening," "Vacuuming" in *Cimarron Review*, July 1995, no. 112; "La Jolla" in *Cimarron Review*, April 1997, no. 119. "Ashfall Fossil Beds" in *College English*, 1997, vol. 59, no. 4. "Acoustics" in *The Cream City Review*, 1997, vol. 21, no. 2. "Beauty," "Felix Culpa," "Mother's Dresser Drawer," "Once Only," "Piano Practice," "Saturn Through a Telescope" in *Iowa Woman*, Summer 1991, vol 11, no. 2. "Jacks" in *Laurel Review*, 1993. "Under Grandmother's House" in *Nebraska Review*, Fall/Winter 1993, vol. 21, no. 1. "November 1963" in *Potpourri*, July/August 1994, vol. 6, no. 7. "The Rapture: Dog Day Cicadas" in *Prairie Schooner*, Fall 1996, vol. 70, no. 3. "Equilibrium of Lily Pads," "Preservation," "These Baptizing Waters" in *South Coast Poetry Journal*, June 1994, no. 17. "Arrivals and Departures" in *Thema*, Autumn 1992, vol. 5, no. 1. "First Frost," "Old Woman Speaks of Thaw" in *Voices on the Landscape*, Michael Carey, editor, Loess Hills Books (Farragut & Parkersburg: 1996).

I am grateful to the Minnesota Voices Project for its support of emerging writers and to Publisher Bill Truesdale and Executive Director Phyllis Jendro of New Rivers Press for their efforts in producing and marketing this book. Special thanks go to Managing Editor Jim Cihlar, whose calm professionalism, courtesy, good humor, and responsiveness made the publication process a pleasure. I am indebted to Briar Cliff College for granting me the sabbatical during which many of these poems were conceived. I am deeply grateful to my fellow writers Tricia Currans-Sheehan, Ginny Duncan, Deb Freese, Phil Hey, and Marlene VanderWiel for their support, encouragement, and constructive criticism; to my editor Connie Wanek and her husband Phil Dentinger for their thoughtful response to my manuscripts; and most especially to my husband Adam Frisch and our children, Eleanor and Austin, for their constant love and belief in me.

Part I

Piano Practice

Your small fingers seek the keys,
your small fingers feeling all over
for the chords, stumbling back over
"Go Tell Aunt Rhodie" again and again,
your small fingers worry the flat tongues,
ordering them to go tell her, to go
tell her over and over, they stammer,
they cannot tell what.
While I in the kitchen
with my hands among the dishes
feel the back of my neck go hard
with the hearing of it. And still
your fingers tense and stiffen, groping
for the gray goose, the old gray
goose . . . the old . . . the old gray goose
is . . . the old gray goose . . . the old. . . .

Your hands smack the keyboard, hard,
and I charge in with my dishrag and
my tongue, so sharp you snap, a long
thin wire wound too tight, now curling
into yourself. Your small shoulders
begin to labor now in perfect time,
more measured than a metronome, more true.

I hold you with my damp hands. My heavy
head rests on your bent head, and I
drink in the smell of your hair, the
smell of boy. And I long to hear
the old gray goose honking unevenly,
strutting and backtracking on the
keys that open nothing, really, but are
only the place of change, where,
for a moment, something that moves,
a pressure, becomes a kind of music.

These Baptizing Waters

We are at the thin brink that marks
indoors and out, you on the high ladder
and I between the glass and the sheer
curtain of the upstairs window.
Our gloved hands circle, a single swan
riding its own reflection.
Like Pisces, we face both ways.

We lean and tilt in the always moving
sun, in whose slant the suspended
smudges are so patently still.
With old diapers, newspapers,
scraps we barely recognize,
we rub until the window fairly brims
with apparent hardness.

And I am remembering that glass
is a liquid, but so viscous, so slow,
that even in this seventy-year-old house
the windows have not yet begun to flow
over the sills. A faint waviness, it may be,
ripples behind the drapes we draw
each night, but that is all.

Then you stretch for a corner,
and the ladder flexes and shifts
beneath your body's weight.
My legs ache in sympathy. I am all
emptiness. There is a moment
when, to stop your fall, I would
put my hand through the cataract
frozen brittle between us.

But you do not fall.
Instead, through the barely visible
striations of the pane, your eyes
widen to mine. You take a breath,
and the window flattens like the skin
of a lake at evening when the wind dies.
The glass gives a long sag and spills
to fluency, to this hard-pouring light,
these baptizing waters.

The Love Poem

I kept my silence,
because the sky lay down
on the wet grass,
weightless and damp against
the cool green of its skin,
because the sky knew
the grass intimately,
so that the grass perspired
with their togetherness,
all its blades erect.

If there had been
an impression of substance,
if the concrete birdbath
had not reflected a birch tree,
the spider's silk
not been suspended
across the open gate,
nor the hummingbird's wings
beaten into transparency—
if there had not been a hammock
studded with leaves,
then there would have been
a place for words to lodge.

And even so,
I cast the net of my poem,
full of emptiness
where silence pours
past knots of language
and leaves behind these scaled fish,
then drains back into the logos,
which, for answer, runs its tongue
over and over the lip of the land.

dead
a fish

controlling
principle of
all life

things all
to get the
heart of
nature

Jacks

For Eleanor

First you lag. Kneeling on the pavement
with the jacks in your palms,
you toss them up and catch them
on the backs of your hands.
They will be light and cold.
Now loft them again and catch them,
the way you would catch water
pouring from a faucet, letting none
spill. This is done in the rhythm
of a spondee. Lag, lag.

Now this is onesies. Scatter them
wide, so the fingers can pluck
each one in the brief interval
when the red rubber ball hangs there
like dawn, defying gravity.
This is twosies and threesies.
Or, for variation, try pigs in a poke,
sheep over the fence, eggs in a basket,
around the world, and no bouncey.

You can play alone or in groups with
others taking their turns. It is also good
to have someone in the background
jumping rope. The rope will slap
the pavement, covering the inaudible
bouncing. Your fingers will snake around
in that space with the ball airborne,
scooping fivesies, sixsies to store
in the cup of your hand, where they
lie weightless as the heads of clover
you would gather to make a chain.

You can play with stones or with
apricot pits, like the Egyptian girls.
Can you see them sitting in the shadow
of the Sphinx? They toss the dry brown
seeds high, because it is always
no bouncey. And the Roman daughters,
they played with bones, little Tertia
and Secunda out on the terrace,
casting those knuckles and hearing
the slap of the Mediterranean, counting on it,
their breasts just budding underneath
the folds of their stolae, while Prima
sauntered under the pines, above it all,
imagining her head on some boy's brown shoulder.

For allsies you ease them down
in a huddle so tight you can grasp it
with your whole hand, the way you
would like to take hold
of everything, a round handful

tight in the fist, with nothing falling
and nothing in front of your knees,
nothing but the hot, white flagstones.

Poppies Opening

The poppies droop their buds,
which are heavy and oval,
like the heads of babies or old men,
compact and perishable,
with that aureole of white fuzz.
Before long, a tear appears,
a bit of red spills out.

And then it is all over. They cannot be contained,
no more than scarves wadded in the fists of magicians can,
nor the laundry of courtesans, tumbled onto their beds
with a softness so astonishing that,
for a moment, the wind ceases to blow.

The Maraschino Cherries in the A&P

were in squat, glass bottles, round and red
as lipstick the tongue has just gone over.
They were lined up on a shelf near Mother's legs,
shinier and redder than anything I had ever
seen before that Saturday. Those balls
of scarlet blew me kisses, while Mother stood
beside the coffee grinder, watching her small
red bag fill up with Eight O'Clock, and I could
not keep myself from asking, so I did.

It seemed a miracle when she said yes.
Maybe she had matters on her mind more
important than the cherries were, or else
she had made love with Father the night before,
and cherries seemed a small thing to ask.
But, for some reason, I did not know what,
she reached down and took one of the glass
jars and twisted the lid, which made a pop,
and gravely held it out. Don't spill, don't drop.

How could she know that first time she gave in
that I would never pass by cherries again
but they would seem already to be mine?
Forget the canned, creamed corn, the Ovaltine,

the wax beans, olives, peaches, pickled beets.
The cherries were for me, the way their sweet
skin would give way between my baby teeth
with a luscious crunch. All other tastes were beneath
contempt. My fingers dipped again and again,
each time dyeing a deeper, redder stain.

Proud and ceremonial, down the aisles
I carried that little bottle like some chalice.
At the check-out, while the cash register bells,
the change, and Mother's purse made metallic
high sounds, snapping and clinking and ringing,
I drank every drop of the juice, tipping the jar.
And I knew then that, though I liked the string
handle, and though the box was a circus car,
it was never going to be animal crackers again,
and the world was in the reach of my hand.

Vacuuming

Saturdays I live for an hour inside this bellowing
that silences children's voices and mutes the jazz quartet
gesturing through my speakers like a brassy salesman
on the other side of the storm door.

I drag the machine by its serpentine nose,
and it churns its belly into a hungry nothing,
all gullet, sucking at the lips of paradise,
emptying noise and silence into its hollow whine.

I am a thief of words. I whirl them like chaff,
and they disperse in this wind, till I am all bereft,
not a trace left, not a sloughed cell, nor tuft of fur,
no gathering dander, paper bits of wrappers,

no grains tracked from the garden, nor fluffs
of dust that shift in drafts. All the soft,
withered residue of life's tree is lofted
into the bag, with crumbs of clandestine meals,

feathers from pillows, the drift of thought,
and the griefs forever sifting themselves
as leaves fallen to mulch are raked in piles
which stir, as if remembering.

A flick of the toe clears the air, and in the immaculate silence
the parakeet screeches from his cage in an ecstasy of answering.
A horn jives through the stereo (wah, wah, wah, wah).
It is the very bugle call of Gabriel, and this is the last day!

La Jolla, 1943-1993

Here in the cove at La Jolla
we sun our fortyish bodies,
where once as newlyweds my parents
played in the water and posed.
The proof is pressed in an album
full of black corners and private
quarters, upon which as a child
I would quietly trespass,
my hands letting in the daylight.
So from time to time their faces
would squint from the tiny windows
against which they were flattened
and beam those steady, uncomprehending
smiles on my shifting self.

Their sunlight must have drifted on,
pumping through the dark spaces
like Heraclitus's bright current.
When I try to conjure her laughter,
his strong arms, there they are,
definite in black and white,
but formal, as tuxedoes are formal,
crisp as clerical collars.
One breath, and they dissolve

into the turquoise waves heaving
and swooning down over the rust-
colored rocks, the great Pacific
dragging its limber grasses back and forth,
green on green, under the yellow sun.

Look. A diver falls to his knees
beneath his tank. Foam is ruffling
his flippers. A bodysurfer torpedoes
toward the rocks. Wet children
squeal and chatter in the permutations
of the water's edge. Here at La Jolla,
Proteus is always grasping and forgetting
the future, taking and losing shape
in the waves, which the cove nevertheless
embraces, as if to keep a kind of faith.

Nothing keeps. These rocks are carved
with the initials of last year's lovers,
all the old confidences long since
divulged to wind and surf. Somewhere
a proud corporal, a careless girl,
whisper their love, but their voices
are lapsing and lapsing under the waves
like something slipping the cove's mind.

Even if I could summon them,
their eyes would pass over me
the way the pelican's shadow
slides up the sand, absorbed
in the love that will one day
engender me. We live forward,
into the wind, while they rock

in our wake like buoys,
shivering and frolicking
inside the dark margins,
where my mother reclines
in my father's arms, her back
to the horizonless sea, like a bride
being carried over a threshold.

Morning Glories

I have started them in flats, from a few
seeds so hard you have to score the outer
casing with a knife, their hulls so dry
you have to soak them in water, waiting
a day to plant them. Some years not one
seedling could take the shock of even a slight
drop in temperature, though I hardened
them off before putting them in the ground.
I moved them out by day and in by night.

This year they take the trellis, curlicue
of tendril, heart-shaped leaf. The bud utters
a sudden gasp of blue. Those dry,
hard seeds smoulder like pipes, germinating
at last, and spinning slender streams of vine
to coil and fume like hookah dreams, with bright,
cool puffs of bloom, so tender you think they'll burn
in the noon sun. Like small umbrellas, unbound,
they unfurl fantastically in the rainless light.

They will not be gathered. They hoard their blue.
In sky or lapis lazuli, there's no other
blue like that. Their deep, drowsy eyes
open, cool and remote, the pupils dilating

yellow and more yellow in the dangerous sun.
They dawn and dawn, until they seem bright
purses gaping, with their linings turned
out, unabashed, each offering that single, round,
unmourning coin, a gift, a widow's mite.

But counterfeit. This inbred, alien hue
is studied, is all art. No blessed mother
ever wore this unvirgin blue. They deny
like high-priced whores, practiced, immaculate in
their cold openness. And, though undone,
like silk underthings astray in early light,
they twist themselves at noon into nocturnal
spirals, and sleep unmoved all day, wound
in pale sheets, spare as shepherd's purse, and tight.

The Genesis of a Poem

It probably will begin with something like an orange,
the roundness of it, perhaps, or the look of it
on the blue plate on the blue and white plaid tablecloth.
And then I might raise my eyes to a man with black hair,
graying, stirring his coffee, who might be my husband,
or a guest who has stayed overnight,
a friend, a stranger, it would be up to me.

I might take up a paring knife and slice the orange,
cutting its seeds plainly, so that they show new surfaces,
white and flat. Or I might, instead, peel it with my thumb
and divide it into sections, and cleanly pull skin from skin,
to share with the man across the table, leaving behind
the rind and the white webbing on the blue plate.
In that case, I will carry the scent of the orange
all day long underneath my nail, and that may be all.

Part II

Acoustics

In the ancient amphitheatre at Epidaurus,
the least whisper is audible, hissing up
concentric rows of benches, under a sun
so hot the air shimmies over the stone.

We scale the steep rake to the very rim
and sink down under the olives' shade.
The cicadas' buzz sloshes from ear to ear,
and our skulls have the feel of baked bowls.

Far below, another man and woman
sit by the flat disk, where diminutive workmen
prepare the stage for tomorrow's *Agamemnon*,
laying a canvas floor the color of blood.

The man says, in English, "The passion has vanished."
His voice sweeps to our ears. "Divorce," he says.
Like lizards rushing for cover the syllables skitter
over the rocks. The olives whisper *hush*.

"You no longer know me. The love is gone."
The words keep pealing up the marble rings
and, as if his tongue has stung her, she shrinks down
and murmurs, "You're wrong." He leans closer.

He bends to her bowed head, her hunched back.
He kisses her. She does not raise her head.
The broken circles surround them as ripples of water
flee the place where a flung stone has sunk.

Is it all those centuries, all those rehearsals,
that give his voice its pitch, her silence its volume?
It seems their hearts have been slow-fired in a kiln,
hardened, fused to the ancient masks of anguish.

Something in these scorched stones magnifies
their private grief into the common ache.
So we grip each other's hands, and the cicadas
shriek, *Clytemnestra, Clytemnestra!*

Arrivals and Departures

At the last bend of the jetway,
    the Houston damp beat once against
    the crisp climate of the air-conditioned
        airport, which rang like a cymbal
           in the chest, and I knew you,
              the pitch of your torso,
                your graying hair still tangled,
            your soft eyes with new scores
        radiating like the splines of a fan,
      your body composed around its central self,
  a bobbin layered around the spindle. And,
in turn, you knew me, your face brightening
    lifting to laughter, your arms out,
        one short embrace unwrapping
           those years wound up in other lives,
              knitted up by day and nightly unraveled
           in the canon we fabricated in our heads.
    With loosening and tightening strains, we
  stitched toward this fugal clasp and letting go.
But there was something unrecognized,
    something the years made, or, perhaps,
        it was always there, waiting to be
           acknowledged through the whispered secrets,
              the incontrovertible trust, laid down behind us.

Some snarled thing, a skein left too long
in the drawer, something you want to take
the end of and pull to free it, and wind up
with a tighter knot, around which you
neatly bind the loose yarn, to keep,
someday to construct you know not what.
What Penelope knew at her loom.
What Daedalus glimpsed beforehand,
pressing those feathers into the soft wax.
What Theseus had forgotten, arriving
with his black sails, though he thought
he had unwound, coil by coil,
every inch of Ariadne's proffered string.

Equilibrium of Lily Pads

Our canoe slices through green cells, unseals
the water briefly. They slip aside, like skin
opening under a knife. Then the dark slit
closes behind us, the surface tension heals.
They are unperturbed, openhearted, their green
a deep coolness risking blue in its shying
from yellow, the limber rounds extended, lying
taut as the stretched horizons we move between.

But our passage rocks them. On each pad a quiet
water bead stirs and begins to roll from side
to side like mercury, shivering into a riot
of silver seeds that circle, slow, and merge,
then quiver to stillness. The leaf is magnified
at the low place where the radiant veins converge.

Mother's Dresser Drawer

There was something hidden in it,
just beneath the scent of Tabu.
It whispered to me from the pink folds
of satin pockets where she kept her stockings.
I would look for the secret passwords
flashing in code: a rhinestone tiara,
a box of baby teeth, single earrings,
pink and gold, envelopes with letters
beginning "Dearest," but these I did not read.

There was a silk bag, beaded, with a chain.
Inside its slippery lining, a program,
a tissue with a lipstick O, and a folded
speech I'd seen her practice over and over
in front of the mirror, memorizing
every lilt and pause, while the glass
gave back the watchful look of her eyes.

Within of within, holy of holies,
most secret, sweet, mysterious, most open,
my mother's dresser drawer.
Like a scroll it unrolled for me,
and solemnly I translated, following
with my fingers, moving
my lips to the ancient language.

And there, above the fullness of it,
the mirror where, like her, I practiced my part,
crowned with rhinestones, wreathed in scarves,
perfume behind each ear, and my lips smeared
with "real, real red," leaning into the dresser drawer
that no one said I was not to open.

Like the one that slides open now for you,
my daughter. I find you standing on tiptoe,
peering over its edge, the edge of the world.
There is a hidden scent you will never identify,
that weighs down all those silly trinkets
your small hands stir, your eyes study.
It is yours. I give it all to you,
all the sunken treasures in the great sea,
tumble upon tumble, brought to the surface for you,
pouring brine, shining under the whole sky.

Ashfall Fossil Beds

Once, long ago, in what is now Idaho,
puffs of volcanic ash spewed up
into a calm, uncontemplated sky,
smoke signals panting for interpretation.
They smeared across the blue, erased the sun,
and lazed over the mountains to this hill
where we stand in what is now Nebraska.

A motley company converged here,
camel, three-toed horse, tufted crane,
rhinoceros, a sort of peaceable kingdom.
They lapped at the thickening gray mud
of a watering hole and gagged, while dust
descended like powder on inked scripture,
blotting the page, bringing a consummation.

They must have fallen to their knees, but not
to utter prayers, who had no thought of God.
They slumped and perished. The white ash sifted
over the humps of their bodies and smothered them
in a snow so silent, so deep, their bones lay
for millennia, just so, like an unread oracle,
desiccated entrails on an abandoned altar.

It took ten million years before an eroded
cornfield yielded up its secret roots,
the fine print in the prairie's lexicon.
A convex lens magnified the velvet
dust, disclosed the microscopic shards
that sliced their lungs, an etymology
too deep, too razor-sharp for the mind to touch.

The hushed brushes sweep away the ash
the way scribes paint ideograms. The ribs
bend parallel, redundant as practice strokes.
The punctuated S-curves of the spine
link the broad bones of the pelvis
to the sphere of the skull, those solemn cavities
where life is first expressed, knowledge uttered.

An infant's skull nuzzles the ribs of its mother.
The bones of a foetus lie like a tiny convict,
locked in a pelvic cell, sending unreadable
letters home, hieroglyphic cartilage,
quill scratches, dainty death sentences,
unstruck matchsticks under a pile
of cold, gray, unilluminating logs.

A barn was built over these bales of bone,
to store the marrowless, unholy families,
ripened, dried, chaff-forsaken, and thwarted,
cropped in their prime. We, too, take shelter here
from an August sun. We shake our heads. We snap
griefless, photosensitive illusions
and drive home to compose blank verse.

You can't help thinking of Auschwitz, Bergen-Belsen,
those stacks of bodies, gray, parchment thin.
You feel a cavern gape inside the ribs
where the heart hides out, a grief uncalled for here,
for who can be blamed but time? Nevertheless,
the flesh of our hands where we take hold of things
seems excessive, inessential now.

I once saw a plastic bag quivering like a skin
against a barbed wire fence. I thought the wind
needed only to die down for it to fall.

Saturn Through a Telescope

Like pilgrims we came, from our separate spaces,
from homework on the kitchen table,
from the typewriter and the television,
called to the lawn behind the house,
where we stood fidgeting in the dark,
waiting for a look at the sky, until, by turns,
again and again we bent and peered and,
through the scope's narrow cylinder,
took in Saturn, like a breath held
too long in the chest. We watched while
it slid out of view, oddly domestic,
a porcelain cup and saucer on a lacquered table.

We stepped back to crane our necks at the sky
and drank in the Milky Way, which flowed
down over us with its stars round and pure,
like the seed pearls on a bridal veil.

The neighbor children came to look,
each taking a turn at the eyepiece, at
the flat white disc that kept dissolving
into the winey sky. And the awestruck
tongue cleaved to the roof of its mouth.

The grass grew wet to drench our shoes,
and someone's mother called from two doors
down. And then, inside, in the lighted room,
we drew the children's baths, aware of the
window where the streetlamp seemed too bright.
They will sleep uneasy, I was thinking,
with this white paper cutout pasted
on the sky like a haloed saint.
And will their knees always ache
in memory of the damp ground
where they knelt once to light
a votive in the cavernous dark?

The Rapture: Dog Day Cicadas

A solitary ticking like a reel
reaches out, quickens, fetches them in
with a high beseeching, and they heed and come,
to breed and creak, and ratchet up the night,
each to each: "Be ye, be ye, be ye."

Their wings fold over their bodies like the tents
of the Israelites, anticipating Zion.
The night aches with the beat of their bellies.
Their membranes shiver and throb with sex hunger
like the drumheads of agitated tribes.

And for seven years everything has been
only a readying for this new issue,
every emergence, every parturition,
a hatch, a wicket, beckoning this way,
in the direction of this wordless creed.

For this, their vacant mothers strained the saws
embedded in their abdomens, to gouge
a single slit into a living twig.
They stretched their bodies to express pearls,
each contraction a prospect, "be ye, be ye."

For this the tender nymphs grew white and fat,
fought their way out of the bulging spheres,
dropped soundlessly, like manna, to the ground,
dug underneath and, year after year,
lay low and softly sucked at the toes of trees.

For this they were unearthed, like Lazarus
dragging his winding sheets. They worked upwards,
climbing the bark to unremembered branches,
affixed themselves, and exited at last,
trailing wings, like brides from limousines.

And now the old skin is left behind,
an onion peel, a flake of arid parchment,
a fluttering leaf, a scroll the scribe left blank.
The land of milk and honey crooks its finger,
and the females twitch and jitter in the shadows.

So it is that, when evening cools around them,
one recollects himself, contracts his timbal,
and rattles out these dry solicitations.
And all their eyes, simple and compound,
dilate in the gray light's waning.

They buzz with Zion-greed. They strain to reach
into the dark to meet his pitch. The air
pulses and pleads, "be ye, be ye, be ye,
be ye lift up, ye everlasting doors!"
They raise their heads a notch, and each and each
unfolds four wings to flee to Paradise.

Heavy Air

To my son

Your adolescent fury is spending itself on Mozart.
The rush of your fingers on the keys
in a currency of chromatics, changes, checks,
a frenzy of Rimsky-Korsakov,
the bee swarm of your bitten nails.
I think I have lost you to music.
I blindly feel for you in the strain,
the drum-buzz of the air.
My heart is a tympani, my ears tambourines.

I close my eyes and scale
the Escherlike stairs of Bach for you,
pitched upside down and sideways,
circulating through the sound you make.
Where is the heart that beats at the center?
The head that storms the room?

When you are done, you are cool and quiet,
hunching back to your closed door.
The house rights itself and finds its gravity.
I tell myself that bonds mature
in silence like this, bass notes, so low

in frequency and altitude, they're inaudible.
I sip coffee from a China cup.
I read a magazine. But I am unstrung.
In my mind I am running up the stairs after you,
tapping on the snare of your bedroom door.

Oil Slick

It surges from us, rhythmic, like a corrupt
pulse, clouding the depths, a greasy stain,
pouring out of a rudely opened vein
and blossoming in the suicidal tub.

It billows out like mad Ophelia's gown,
which for a moment buoyed her up, still singing
her aimless song, then, with her fist clinging
to the wilted bunch of flowers, dragged her down.

The surf heaves up and paws and slaps its hands.
It pants like a drunken lover. Afterwards
it pulls back, leaving bruises, bodies of birds,
blackened lumps clotting the inert sand.

A cormorant moves beneath a robe of sludge,
dragging a crude drapery on his wings,
which weighs upon him like the gabardine
of an academic, clergyman, or judge.

And on the water there's a bright chain
of dying fish. They stiffen, soften, and bloat,
while dolphins slide into new black coats
and shine like hearses cruising in the rain.

So all the innocents move in the slow sea,
bobbing in the currents, load on load,
hauled outward by the driven undertow,
heron, turtle, grebe, and manatee.

Under Grandmother's House

Beneath the house of my father's childhood,
out of the Louisiana sun, we cousins sat
in our summer shorts, hunched under the rough-
lumbered floor joists, burying our hands.
With the bowls of Grandmother's spoons we scraped
the ground down to the darker, cooler dirt
that would mold around a cupped hand.

There beside the brick pilings that held
the house up above us we heard the grown-ups
walk in their Sunday shoes, setting the table.
My aunt's high heels knocked back and forth
on the linoleum-covered planks. We sat wordless
beneath all that talk, all that work above the joists,
the governor's race and the Southern Baptist Convention,
and biscuits rolled on the floured board. Browning
and socialism and the clatter of dishes washed,
and the silence of the leftovers in their bowls,
covered with their white cotton cloths.

We held our breath, flattening our fingers,
drawing them out slow, without the least tremble,
that they would leave behind the little hollows
where we'd ease the bristly balls we'd gathered
from underneath the sweetgum trees.

On all sides the long rectangles of light blazed.
The nervous white chickens stretched
their necks and pecked at the rinds of
watermelons left from Sunday dinner.
We heard the slow drag of Granddaddy's broom
hissing across the floor of the front room
where we'd banged in and out of the screen door
all day long, tracking in the sand.
And we sat there digging in the dimming
shadow of the house heavy above us, making
mounds out of the earth with our small hands,
until the voices rang to call us up into the light.

And there under an incandescent bulb we would huddle
in the deep, rust-scented water of the claw-footed tub,
rubbing ourselves slippery with sweet soap.
The dirt from our feet went round and round
into the deep drain. And past the window screen,
out in the cricket-loud night, we could feel
how the ragged trunks of the cedars gathered
the coolness around their shoulders like a shawl.

Then we lay watching the waterstains on the ceiling,
crowded like eggs in mattresses that sagged,
in the smooth sheets, in nightgowns of batiste,
in the rustle of the sycamore trees, with our clean hands
curled on grandmother's quilt, while underneath us,
where the moon could not reach, the small barrows
whose walls still bore the imprint of our fingers
dried and crumbled, grain by grain, in the night breezes.

Part III

Preservation

This afternoon we walked the rise
and fall of the land, beneath a hue
and cry of blue sky and blackbirds.
In a deep hollow the early frost missed
we found a single yellowing ash, draped
with the vines of wild grapes, which shone
small and dark and knowing, as if the birds
had left their eyes behind to prove
home was a place they could fly to blind.

Then you climbed into the wincing leaves,
my son, pendant, perishable,
like the fruit you reached for.
There was your shoe with the edge
of its sole angled on a loop of vine,
your bucket swinging on your arm.
Your body sagged out, leaning west,
with its brief fingers stretched
to pluck the last cluster.

The leaves huffed in the October wind.
The branches lurched beneath you.
With rough, unmaternal rocking
they held sway, while you took hold

with one hand and your shoe.
My eyes hooked like anchors into you,
and I held my breath
as if that would keep back time.

When you were down, the grapes
rounded into the pail, they were
so few. But as we came out of the shade
toward home, into a field restless with wind,
I knew there were enough to pick through,
crush, boil, strain, sugar, and boil again,
for this one pint of savage jelly,
which we will eat at Christmas, maybe,
famished for the fierce tang of autumn
and a single day, pending snow, pending
dark, on the featheredge of gathering.

The Cat in the Park

If the cat had dragged himself into the cannas,
he would have died there quietly, unexposed.
He would not have been in the open as he was,
in front of the statue of Lincoln, gray as the mist,
and still, as if an inscription ought to be chiseled
into the softness of him. Then the wrongness of it
would not have stopped my walk the way it did.

If was only a light mist. His fur was drenched.
Not five feet away there was dry ground
under the heavy, broad leaves of the cannas.
I knew then that it must be hopeless with him.
No cat lies willingly in the wet.
I sat on the grass. The damp seeped through my jeans.
Back and forth we spoke in words and mews.
He let me touch him with my cold fingers
deep in his fur, vibrating with his purring.

There was the rapid rise and fall of his breathing,
the rough drag of his licking on the back of my hand.
The fallen leaves of an ash lay bright yellow
on the green grass and, among them, scattered curls
of a peculiar red. Not leaves, it dawned on me,
but petals blown from the cannas, tongues of fire.

First Frost

We bring the pots indoors.
The plants sprawl with the growth
of a full season. The marigolds
gape open, bee-hungry, uncovering
all their ruffled slips.

We unfold every last sheet
to drape the tenderest vines.
The pretense of modesty alone
ought to spare their sweet skins.

Come morning, we set
the earthen pots outdoors
again and let the flowers
resume their wanton intercourse
with every flying thing.

We drag the damp linens
off the vegetables, which lie
twined around each other,
naked and unblinking
under the oblique sun.

The last fruits dawdle to maturity.
Zucchini lengthen to what end?
Potatoes quietly fatten underground.
While we bustle with the bedclothes
and talk incessantly, like Juliet's nurse,
the squashblossoms swoon open once again,
and lift their yellow crinolines
for love, for love, for love.

Fence

*Upon the death of fifteen wallabies and their offspring
at The Henry Doorly Zoo, Omaha, November 1992*

1.

Outside the locked enclosure of the wallabies,
where even paying visitors are forbidden,
three dogs, unwashed, collarless, unlicensed,
pace back and forth, nails clicking on the pavement.
From between their uncivil jaws breath-puffs steam.
Their tongues hang. Their snarls gurgle and rise
to a moon-fed cry. Out of the ancient blood
of their sires' sires, out of savannas unearthed,
ranges undreamed of, certain memories form.
So they lunge and lunge against the south fence.

2.

Deep in their mothers' pockets, the little ones
suckle. Their delicate eardrums pick up barking,
the quickened heartbeat, the panicked ticking.
They sense the speed and suddenness, borne up
in such long arcs, such jarring descents
that they curl up tight inside their warm pouches,
like fists inside the bloodied gloves of boxers.
No wonder their skulls crack, thin as eggshells,

when the wallabies cast themselves on the north fence.
They break each others' bones and crush the young,
pressed in that tight, incomprehensible stasis.

3.

Two bald primates arrive, bipeds, sighing
and shaking their heads under the cold stars.
Such bloodless carnage. Not a tooth touched hide.
While one counts: fifteen adults, eight joeys
(his hand closing over the warm bodies),
the other creeps up to the plunging dogs
(whose hoarse barks are raising maddened replies
from nearby inmates—wolf, coyote, dingo—
but citizens of Omaha, all the same),
and seeing the dogs are feral, merely strays,
he hefts up his shotgun to his shoulder
and brings them to a human kind of justice,
raising the dead to an even twenty-six.

Delivery

Bub will let you take your sweet time picking
through the merchandise. Those frames
surrounding winged children, with their flaking
gilt and the blue women with their golden chains
from which sacred hearts dangle like valentines.

You can handle the glass—Bub won't mind—
pressed, cut, depression, carnival,
colored, water, clear—etched with sand—
or opaque—bits of pottery, porcelain,
stoneware, graniteware, earthenware.

You will see a boudoir chair with rose
brocade upholstery, torn, divulging wads
of tangled horsehair making a slow escape.
A brass floor lamp with a busted shade
wobbling on a cracked marble base.

A vanity with the mirror going dark,
rippling veneer, joinery coming loose—
dovetail, dado, mortise and tenon,
rabbet—all working themselves free,
shrinking and swelling, letting go of their glue.

Resurrected from some chest of drawers,
a photo album none of the family wanted
lies open on a water-spotted table,
exposing all those cracking prints
of people who knew better than to smile.

And through it all, embedded like fossils,
that indistinguishable dust, the soft trace
of more than one devout mother,
sitting erect at her dining room table,
presiding over a Sunday ham.

You can see her capable hand cupped
around the relish dish as she lifts and passes
the yellow and red and green of the succotash
that was the last of the garden, and the pickles
made from August watermelon rinds.

You can see her with her smooth arms lifted up,
her back to the beveled glass of her dresser,
crimping her hair with the iron. She holds
a bone-handled mirror in which she eyes
the reflection of the reflection of the back of her head.

You can see her in her husband's chair,
overstuffed and doilied, suddenly
relinquishing herself to laughter.
She rocks back, her hands against her stays,
her youngest child sliding from her lap.

And the creaking sound you hear may be the chair
or the stays, or Bub, shifting his weight,
but before your eyes, her sloughed cells rain

onto the weave you stroke and appraise,
received into the fabric without comment.

Bub, too, is a man of few words,
nodder at auctions, gleaner of goods discarded,
fallen by the way. We deliver, he says.
In time you will succumb, if only to buy
a linen someone embroidered in the spring.

Snow Geese at DeSoto Bend

The Missouri twists below them
like a strip of discarded aluminum,
and they follow its bright curves to this one bend,
where some primal memory bears them down
to float in place on the water or hunker
in the yellow grasses for weeks and weeks
before they rouse themselves
for the next push south.

From where I stand they litter the water
like tiny rounds of confetti, discrete as petals
beneath spring apple trees after a storm.
But, let the eye blur even slightly,
and they blanket the river like snow on floes.
The month is November, but the river
flows both ways, out of the present.

The sun lowers, and as if by the silent signal
of some anointed prophetbird,
or by a deep consensus
inside their collective hunger,
they flap up, dry leaves in the wind,
and are blown downriver,
four hundred and forty thousand in all.

They fly from the water
the way sparks spiral from a bonfire.
I once saw a jeweler drag a diamond bracelet
across dark velvet.
It was like that also, bright and slow.

They make a racket that wrestles down the crowd
of words in me, the honking, and the crooked
wings snapping like sheets on a line.
I want to know what it is that lifts them up
and drags them like the rags on the tail of a kite.

They move in a wedge
as if to force their way into something.
Or perhaps they simply trail each other
as wakes might disturb the water
after the passage of an invisible craft.

I know only that these are the forms
I see in my dreams, small, dark, and bent,
circumflex accents on a red, wingbeaten sky,
the dust of combines ignited in the sun,
a tolling of bells, a benediction.

Felix Culpa

When I came out of the pink morning
into the dark garden,
my back to the ruffled sky,
the antlers of the tree flared
beneath little leaves moving in unison,
and the faces of angels froze in dismay,
for, round in my hand, heavy,
fitting my hand more surely
than the smaller, sweeter fruits of other trees
the pomegranate lay.

And so I swallowed, seed by seed,
and grew full to know
how sorrow would come lashing
through the too-green grass
and the birds go suddenly silent in the trees.

I think often, with regret,
of the ruffled room, populated
with angels and animals
shining pink in the sun.
My ear is cocked always
for the trill of the pretty bird
that flutters on the other side of the shut door.

Even so, I have not once wished
not to have eaten, and again eaten,
and eaten again.

November 1963

We had always relied
on the self-containment of heads,
but, in spite of us, the bullets
entered, the same way knowledge
ripped through Eden,
exposing everything.

In the glass of the television screen
the miraculous pixels swarmed,
and they buzzed into the holes
of our eyes and ears, humming
in the round coherences
of our innocent skulls,
our palms cupped around them,
prayerful, unbelieving, until,
like fireflies in a jar,
they went dark from being
brought inside into the light.

The red on Jackie's pink suit
broke our hearts like a valentine
sent to somebody else. We watched
her hold up her dark head under
the pillbox hat. We saw her children

reaching to her gloved hands.
Jealously, we crept behind her grief,
into the shadow of her black veil,
twisting light like a dragonfly wing.

We have always locked hands,
we who were fourteen then.
I think we were all fourteen,
brash, pubescent, vulnerable,
straddling that breach, holding
our hands on our heads the way
the earth's crust floats on its magma,
the plates of our skulls seismic
with the pressure of what has
forced its way in.

Is it any wonder our faces zipped
shut, tight as body bags,
our eyes red with the smoke of grass,
late nights, tear gas, feeling time
slope up toward that moment and fall
away again, a jag of mountain that can't
help but be the center of something?

We still hear those thuds:
a copper-cased Junebug
jarring the window screen,
or a moth battering the light bulb,
or the soft, dark body of the bat,
breathing with its little lungs,
faint in the fold of the drape.

Once Only: Austin Snow

I saw you that way, late afternoons, always
over the rim of a glass of beer. We'd talk,
the change growing on the table between us.
They kept the shutters closed, but through the chinks
yellow beams would float across the space
above your face.

Only once, as we stepped out into the night,
there came a miraculous snow, and I glanced back
and saw you opening your umbrella, black
against the whiteness that raged out of the night,
the soft, fierce flakes coursing around,
bringing the darkness down.

And there we stood astonished, feathered with snow,
after the shutters and the amber glow,
beneath the same umbrella, holding tight
to each other's hands, as if the golden light
had had nothing to do with the beer, as if the sky
had torn open beneath the mysterious, high
mating of a swan and some god of the night.

Trimming the Christmas Tree, After Your Mother's Stroke

We are looking for a small tree. If we stand it
on a table in your mother's living room, it should leave
just enough room under the ceiling for the angel
to be contained. This year we are modest
in our expectations. The man drags himself
from his heated trailer and sells us this one
for only ten dollars, crooked as a dog's leg
and sawed from a root left to rot in some field
over spring. Christmas is in two days.

You set the trunk into the stand at an angle,
so that it seems upright. I wedge it in
with broken clothespins and folded cardboard.
Then we prune the limbs. When we are done,
its outline forms an isosceles triangle.
If you didn't know better, you would swear
it was straight, there against the dark window.
But in the day every curvature is backlit.
You can see the trunk weave and right itself,
as your mother swerves and regains her balance.

In the attic cubbyholes are dusty boxes,
full of lights, tangled as old resentments.
This year, like a miracle, they burn,
illuminating the hollows between the branches.
The old glass balls, brittle as our moods,
hang on thin wires. We are doing this
for the children and for your mother and because
there is something we must live up to in ourselves,
a precedent, an inclination toward grace.

For hours we thread popcorn and cranberries
the birds would love, if there were real birds.
But the only feathered things on this tree
are birds with wings dyed red as clots,
their feet wired to the branches, and the suppressed,
ragged angel, trying to announce something
from on high, inaudible as a dog whistle.

To My Daughter on Valentine's Day, Fifth Grade

You were straight and solid and golden
as bamboo or a length of sugar cane.
Now your body's mass shifts
to roundness like a candy heart,
and when I open a door and catch you
naked, you hunch over, your hands spread
to screen yourself, like the fan of a geisha,
your knees bent to one side, as if by turning
you might disappear from view.

You have always had those plum-colored lips,
shaped like a valentine, those bright eyes,
that yellow hair. You have always been
well contained in your body, sure of the world.
These days you spill over, dissolving
to this and that, tears and talk. You fly out,
your anger whirling about you like bees.
You coil into your quiet, a soft mollusk,
backing in, round and round, to rest at the heart.
You have discovered your insides.
You have begun to furnish a room there.

Today you had a valentine from some boy
the other children teased, one you were kind to.
How do I love thee, he wrote, copying out
all fourteen lines into his spiral notebook,
ignoring the breaks, misspelling "griefs."
I have had a crush on you for three years,
he said in his own words. And, though you cringed,
I loved this boy who formed words like "soul"
and "ideal grace," his slow pencil exalting him,
who for that eternity from third grade to fifth,
was occupied with thoughts of my girl, my once
flat green spear of iris, now plumping and purpling
from her gold-dusted depths, piquant, bruisable.

Part IV

Aging Woman Speaks of Thaw

Beneath the bright sky, the snow slumps,
twenty inches of drift undercut
by rivulets of melt. The edge
of the hard-packed white
decays to slush.

The plowed banks settle and sweat
their outer white, uncovering
layer on layer of road grit
like the darkening strata
of the memory's traces.

Outside my window an icicle
salivates, lengthens on the eave.
I am suspended like that,
brittle and longing to let go.

Spruce branches bear snow
the way children trudging home with sleds
wear their sodden sleeves.
They stare at their boots and do not notice
the emaciated snowmen in their front yards,
how they shrink into themselves
and let go of their brooms.

The white poplars
sway beneath their fat, black birds,
openly, as if all along they have known
that burdensome pretense of purity
wouldn't have to be kept up forever.

Though the hair on my head grows white,
my speech blackens and diminishes
to these hard, cold utterances.
My tongue is always coming to some
shattering conclusion or other.
And I know this is how
I am going to grow old.

Beauty

To have it, you must make it,
and then nothing is safe.
Even old Mrs. Barnett's living room
will yield it, under pressure.

Her picture of the Last Supper
was grooved like a phonograph record.
When you walked across the room
it caught the light and shifted
and became Golgotha
above the sofa.

The doilies contributed to it.
It is easy to hold oneself above doilies,
underneath lamps, draped on the arms of chairs.
But doilies are inevitable, eternal.
They make white spots on the periphery of vision
that do not fade.

Her flowers mounted on the wall
paled and gathered dust.
But there is poignancy in plastic,
the way it bends and melts.

Let the petals drop away,
have the fronds lean
toward the host in the center of the frame,
let the eye pace one step to the side,
and feel the crocheted circles
spin on the edge of light.

If you are to have it, it will be got
one way or another
out of rooms such as this, furnished,
composed, illuminated, wrung to clarity.

Plane Geometry

To Miss Vera MacFarland

In front of the blackboard in your plaid shirtwaist,
you'd rock back on your blunt-toed, laced-up shoes,
your belt bouncing above your round belly,
your chin stuck out beneath that horse-toothed mouth,
with your purplish lipstick stretched in a great smile
that showed your gums. "Be lazy, but be lazy
in-tell-i-gent-ly," you'd say, dividing the words
into equal parts, stressing each syllable.
You once measured my skirt with a ruler
and proved it was shorter than two inches above
the midpoint of my knee. You made me go home
and change. Oh, you were strict, Miss Mac.
You'd pat one palm with that big chalk compass,
and warn us, "When you get on college campus,
you're going to go down like the Titanic."
And then you'd be all teeth again, and your gray
permanent wave would curl tight around your face
and your glasses in perfect little circles.

On the blackboard behind you the proofs loomed,
the axes and angles, acute, oblique,
the triangles, isosceles and right,

the parallelograms, cones, cubes,
and those three dots that signified "therefore."
And I want to ask you, Miss Mac, is a line still
an infinite number of points where you are?
And, if so, can you count them every one,
yourself infinite, floating overhead
in your black shoes and plaid and wire rims,
with those spheres about you silently revolving
in elliptical orbits? Have you looked God in the face
with that grin of yours and said "There's more ways
to skin a cat than starting at its hind legs"?
Miss Mac, are you still Methodist? Or did you
go home and change? Are you transfigured?
Do you have circumference? Are you perfected?
Do parallel lines finally meet?

The Bracelet

There she is on the cover of *Time*, cross-legged
on the sub-Saharan desert, her son
lying limp across the legs he once slid between
when her womb squeezed him out,

that now, some years later (ancient-faced),
his head might droop like the bud of a poppy,
on the stem of his neck, the flies on his eyelids
permanent as moles, no one moving to brush them away.

On her wrist is a bracelet of blue beads,
like a tear in her skin where the sky spills out,
finding its own level—her crescent, her oasis,
singing out of the brown land in a familiar tongue.

Her eyes twist to focus me. They iris open,
making holes that light comes through,
like cigarette burns in the pages of *Time*,
which are otherwise flat, quotidian, perishable.

Some jackhammer is drilling through the earth
punching up to where she sits staring at the camera,
her breasts empty against her ribs, her child
in her lap, his belly pregnant with death.

A hole in the ground pulls like a vacuum.
My bones loosen in their sockets and she has me.
Her bracelet is radiant, uranium dense. It burns.
It melts my flesh. We fuse under the merciless sun.

We rotate with death in our laps,
twins tumbling in the womb of God.
The bracelet coils around us, a braid,
wet, umbilical, a rope of clear water.

And we are two hemispheres rolling in space
locked, centrifugal, bound with this belt,
this boundary, this slit of sky, this wound,
this equator, this bright circumference of blue.

What I Have of You

To my grandmother
burned to death, January 1959

I try to hold you as an idea in my head,
the way I would hold a cut-glass bowl,
carefully, with both hands, feeling its mass,
its sharp edges, the pressure of it on my palms,
though it is empty of pickles or spiced apples.

What I have of you is your locket. I slide my nail
between the two halves, to find inside my mother
as a knock-kneed child, and your young husband
whom I never saw, and nothing of you but the picture
behind my eyes, a heart sealed and unhinged.

I have your recipe for fruitcake, dark,
studded with citron and red and green cherries,
through whose thin slices I try to make you out
the way children in church try to make out God
past the colors of those crazy windows, webbed with lead.

The pinafore you basted me for dress-up,
those rotting panels of green and pink cotton.
The ragdoll you made, her face embroidered

crooked and sad, a mask of you, the way
your mind was crooked, the way it was sad.

Those pecan cookies sliding out of my oven,
buttery lumps, shaken with powdered sugar
like the ash on embers, like the hope of something
smouldering under the dust, that might glow
if you stirred it and stand up in tongues of flame.

How they cracked that cat-o'-nine-tails into your brain,
lightning piercing the high, green wind of a twister.
How one chill morning you backed up to the bisque
of a radiant heater, how your nightgown billowed out,
how it glowed and rose and took you home from Oz.

Bloodroot

A single leaf folds
around the closed bud
like a prayerbook shut
on the white forefinger
of a pious young girl.
And then everything opens,
eyes, hands, books,
the green cape thrown off
and the white body emerging,
spinning and swirling her skirts,
and all smile, smile, smile.
But in the dark under the bed,
where nobody can see,
are the red shoes she wears
when everyone presumes she is asleep,
the ones she dances in
until her tender feet bleed.

Easter Hydrangeas

These potted pink hydrangeas
look like three mammoth breasts,
engorged with milk or passion,
flushed and spotted, bruised by kisses,
their multiple nipples erect
as a host of angels.

The least neglect
will make them sag
and bare their greenish undersides
with such abject despair
you have to drench the soil to revive them.

Whereupon
they raise themselves demurely
for the stroke of your eye,
the brush of your nose, a furtive caress.
Is this, I ask you, what we are to think of
on the Resurrection?
Please say yes.

Easter Lily Rag

The blossoms stare in all directions of the compass
swiveling their heads like lighthouse lamps,
emitting conical, white beams.
They listen hugely, like porcelain RCA Victor horns
at right angles to the upright stem.

Their form is so symmetrical, so enlightened, you'd think
they belonged in a garden in Versailles. From each bloom
six stamens issue, tipped with a bead of gold,
and a single pistil like a wire, on which a pale stigma
hangs, vaguely shaped like a freshwater pearl.

They blare out a scent sweeter than anything
has a right to be. It might almost be fear. You'd think
they came out of a painting by Dante Gabriel Rossetti.
So pure, so tense, so white, so open, so alert,
you'd almost think they were present at the Annunciation.

Loess Hills

This hill I stand on is an egg of land
in spring, when the grasses still fold
their blades in such tender dreams
of birth. The leaves come out of the trees,
cowled in green and full of wide-eyed wonder,
like monks rising from prayer. Strange,

how new it seems, year after year. Stranger
how we overlay the changing land
with other springs, transparent, wonderful,
construed in memory, deep and manifold,
so that standing on a hill with grass and trees
is like entering a complicated dream

of the uneasy prairie. Today the dream
is of seasons gone, and I am a stranger
in the year. I recall the summer trees
in their plump petticoats, how they dotted the land
like figures from Seurat, unfolding
their umbrellas on the hill, as if to wander

casually up. Fall ended that. I wonder
how the earth can bear to dream
for centuries this way, moving in its sleep, folding

itself in the soft sift of these strange
impressionable humps of glacial land,
where sumac is always wounding the hill, and trees

germinate, rise up, and die. The trees
have trouble wintering here. It's a wonder
these few survived the ice and deer, while the land
slept deep and hard, muffled like a deaf dream.
In the silence of the snow, the strange,
round hills huddled like sheep in the fold.

One revolution of the planet and it enfolds
the sun in such an embrace, the trees
blushing and undressing in the strange
courtship of earth and sky. Still I wonder
if this minuet that seems the earth's sweet dream
is only my heart breaking over and over, if this land

could ever dance in fourfold roundelay. No wonder
these young ash trees hold aloof as in a dream,
when the eye is always a stranger, longing for a lost land.

The Garden

To Marie Huot, living with cancer

I will not say a divine hand has sown these spores
that sprout in you so suddenly,
the way mushrooms come after rain,
ringing the trees.
I will not say that good will come of it,
or that it was meant to be.

Nor will I say some evil wind
has blown these seeds through your young body
like dandelion silk on summer days.
This may be only a thing life does by accident,
to announce, inadvertently,
how rich it is, and brief.

Tonight I worked on a jigsaw puzzle.
It was a sober hand that strayed
over the fragments in the box.
Your news like leaden marbles
kept rolling and colliding in my head.

I will say that grief guided my fingers.
Every piece I absently picked up,

each leaf and petal and bit of sky,
locked into place, it seemed,
as if the shards of some relic
were furiously crying out to be whole,

as if the world insisted on making sense,
while my mind raced and sorrowed.
This garden that has been planted in you,
with its groping and its tireless sowing,
though my thoughts tend the idea of it,
gravely, lovingly, I cannot make it habitable.

I will say that the deep shade it spreads
makes everything else luminous—
this red carpet my toes dig into,
the steadfast whiteness of the walls,
the distinction of the edge of the table,
the wild, blue lights of the wine glasses,
and you, most of all, with your plans
and your truth-telling, your clarity,
in whom this tangle unfurls, tendril by tendril,
to prune and cut back, to clear the ancient
secret door that opens onto the light.

Rootbound

In April, in the nursery, the impatiens
stood erect, its buds like baby kisses
pursed against her liver-spotted hands,
with promises even spring couldn't be held to,
which, being old, she ignored. Even so,
she took it home and waited for last frost.

Now, in May, she is too tired for digging
and kneeling down on her brittle bones,
but the plant wilts with the least sun, to shame her.
Like a dry sponge in a pail, its rootball
soaks up water, all the while fisting
and tightening in the orange walls of the pot.

Behind her the house squats on its foundation,
fat with chests of doilies and embroidered
antimacassars, starched, pressed, and folded.
Lately it has unnerved her how, year by year,
the photographs of her smiling grandchildren
propagate, effacing the floral wallpaper.

She spreads her knees apart and leans down,
tapping the pot lightly with a trowel. The rootball
comes out whole and round like an infant's head,

all the soil converted to white threads,
and only the beads of vermiculite left
to show there was ever anything but root.

She rolls the tough mass between her palms.
The tiny chains of her mother's necklaces
have clumped in the box into a single knot of silver,
which she massages between her small fingers
till the strands untangle and hang from her hands,
lightly coiling onto the velvet lining.

No, this is the ground they are sinking into,
dark and cool. They rest there, weightless as gauze.
The lacy veil spread out on the old brown
counterpane, like a web, and the seed pearls
Mother fastened on, one by one. Sweet!
She is down on her knees, digging like a dog.

When her fingers press the earth around the stem,
she feels herself lift ever so slightly,
and for that one moment the ache in her knees is gone.
It seems that all of her life has led up to that.
She waters and waters, and the bruised tendrils
moan and stretch themselves like Solomon's wives
opening to receive his dark embraces.

About the Author

Jeanne Carter Emmons was born on October 5, 1949, in Minden, Louisiana. She grew up in Beaumont, Texas, and attended Lamar University and the University of Texas, where she received her BA, MA, and Ph.D. in English. She married Adam Frisch in 1977 and taught briefly as an assistant instructor at the University of Texas. In 1978 she moved to Iowa and has been teaching English and Writing at Briar Cliff College ever since. She has been poetry editor of the *Briar Cliff Review* since its inception in 1989. She won the *Iowa Woman* poetry competition in 1991 and the *South Coast Poetry Review* competition in 1994. Her work has been published in a number of journals, including *Prairie Schooner, Cream City Review, Cimarron Review, Laurel Review, Calyx, Nebraska Review, Christian Century*, and *College English*. Her poems also have appeared in *Voices on the Landscape*, an anthology of Iowa writers edited by Michael Carey. She lives in Sioux City, Iowa, with her husband and her children, Austin and Eleanor.

Mary Gallager
Richard Wilber